STUDIO PRESS BOOKS

First published in the UK in 2017 by Studio Press Books,
an imprint of Kings Road Publishing, part of Bonnier Books UK,
The Plaza, 535 King's Road, London, SW10 0SZ

www.studiopressbooks.co.uk
www.bonnierbooks.co.uk

Printed Under License ©2017 Emotional Rescue
www.emotional-rescue.com

3 5 7 9 10 8 6 4

All rights reserved

ISBN 978-1-78741-207-1

Printed in Italy

The Wit & Wisdom of
WINE

STUDIO
PRESS

While watching some boring TV, Jack and Jean suddenly remembered that they had an unopened bottle of wine left.

Life rule number 74:
Always put your make-up on
before you open the wine.

She usually didn't mind jokey presents, but frankly she thought this was just sick, twisted and morally offensive.

"**I**'ll have the Beef In Red Wine,
please!" she said,
"But easy on the beef."

"Mmmm, I'm getting oat and wheat tinged with a sharp hint of summer," she said. "Really? I'm getting gradually sloshed with an ever-increasing need to wiggle my fun-bags at people!" replied her mate.

You never had to call her.
Simply pop a wine cork
and she came running!

Emma was having her favourite dream... drinking the giant glass of red wine!

Linda invented Shirazercise!

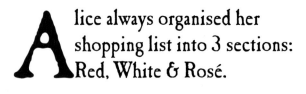

Alice always organised her shopping list into 3 sections: Red, White & Rosé.

She liked to buy her wine, 'Countdown-Style'. She'd take four from the top, three from the middle, two from the bottom, then everyone would guess what jumbled words came out of her mouth.

Emma was a bath person. It was too hard to drink wine in the shower.

"I really do love you, you're my best friend in the whole world!" she said. "Is that the wine talking?" he asked. "No, it's me talking to the wine!"

She was confused – the cookbook clearly said to use leftover wine. "Leftover wine?!"

The Feng Shui harmony in Holly's house was restored once she'd moved the wine nearer to the telly!

"hat's the name of that thing you're ironing on?" she enquired.
"Board!" said her friend.
"Me too!" she replied,
"Let's have a glass of wine!"

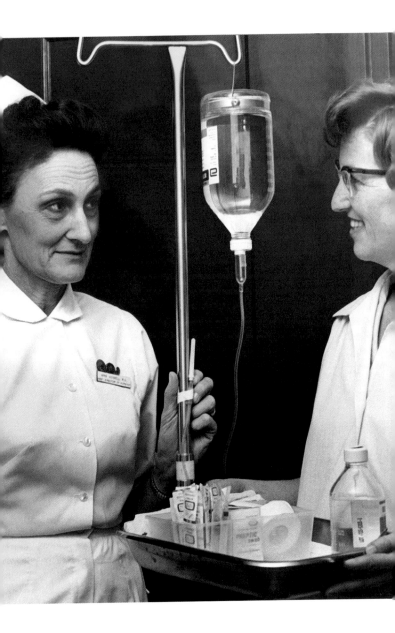

At her request, the birthday girl was about to be hooked-up to a drip full of Pinot Grigio.

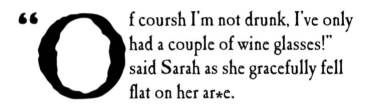

"**O**f coursh I'm not drunk, I've only had a couple of wine glasses!" said Sarah as she gracefully fell flat on her ar∗e.

"A good man can make you feel sexy, strong and able to take on the world," said Helen.
"Oh no, sorry! That's wine... wine does that!"

The others began to suspect Sue was taking her drinking too seriously when she insisted on measuring to make sure no one else had more wine than her.

"**A** little wine, dear?"
"Ok... your driving is sh∗t!"

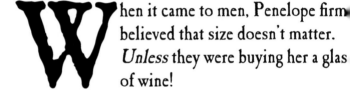

When it came to men, Penelope firmly believed that size doesn't matter. *Unless* they were buying her a glass of wine!

For her birthday, Emma had received a wine stopper. *'Why would anyone ever want to stop the wine?!'*

"I feel like an expensive bottle of wine," she said. "You mean you're improving with age?" he asked. "No," she replied, "It's time I was drunk!"

"If you had to choose between drinking wine every day, or being skinny, which would you choose?" she asked.
"Red or white?" replied her friend.